"Your Faith Will Be Tried and Tested!"

"Your Faith Will Be Tried and Tested!"

"My brethren, count it all joy when you fall into divers temptations."
James 1:2

Dr. R. Michael Baldock

Library of Congress Control Number: 2021911750

PAPERBACK: 978-1-955955-20-1
EBOOK: 978-1-955955-21-8

Unless otherwise indicated all scripture quotations a taken from the King James Version

All Hebrew and Greek definitions are from Strong's Expanded Exhaustive Concordance of the Bible James Strong

Ordering Information:

For orders and inquiries, please contact:
1-888-404-1388
www.goldtouchpress.com
book.orders@goldtouchpress.com

Printed in the United States of America

CONTENTS

INTRODUCTION

<u>**'Your Faith will be Tried, Tempted and Tested!'**</u>

It does not matter where you are at in your walk with God, you will be faced with some kind of trial, test or temptation. The good news is, God has made a way for the believer to make it through every trial, and temptation.

> *"These things I have spoken unto you, that in me ye might have peace. In the world ye shall have tribulation: but be of good cheer: I have overcome the world." John 16:33*

> *"There hath no temptation (trial or test) taken you but such is common to man: but God is faithful, who will not suffer you to be tempted above that ye are able; but will with the temptation also make a way to escape, that ye may be able to bear it." 1 Corinthians 10:13*

There are many important factors involved in this process that every believer will face. In the following pages we are going to address these factors along with the process. There is one very important key to keep in mind. It is important to distinguish the origin of the testing. Keep in mind, God never tempts any man (believer) with evil. Any and all temptations that draws man to do evil and or sin, is orchestrated by Satan and his minions!

The real question is, **'Why?'** Why is it necessary for the believer to face this kind of tests? We are going to answer that question, along with some others within the following pages. That being said, I do not pretend that this book is an exhaustive study on this subject. However, we will investigate different levels of trials, tests and temptations. Keep in mind:

Testing is not for the tester to know where you are in faith (God in this case is the teacher and He already knows where you are in faith)!

When you (the believer) are going through a test, it will reveal your stability or lack thereof in faith! It will also reveal your character along with your attitude. This information, when complete is designed to reveal the things you (the believer) need to improve and grow in! **REMEMBER;**

<u>'UNTESTED FAITH CANNOT BE TRUSTED!'</u>

CHAPTER 1

'Your Faith Will Be Tested!'

**The Questions are;
"Why the testing and what is the purpose?"**

We live in a world of uncertainties. However, there is one thing for certain, YOUR FAITH WILL BE TESTED. YOU WILL FACE OPPOSITION. It is not the test neither the opposition that will stop you. But it is the way you face it, respond to it, act or react to it! The outcome is determined by you! Within the following pages, we are going to examine the temptations, trials and testing, that the believer will face. Within every test, there is a purpose. It is important to note, God never tempts anyone with evil. Those kinds of test originate from Satan himself (James 1:13-15) which we will discuss later.

We will also reveal why it is necessary for the believer to face any kind of testing. But first, let's examine a passage of scripture that deals expressly how to face the tests that come our way!

The great writer James gives very needed instructions as to how we must face the trails and temptations that we will face.

> *"My Brethren, count it all joy when you fall into divers temptation;"*
> *"Knowing this, that the trying of your faith worketh patience,"*
> *"But let patience have her perfect work, that ye may be perfect and entire, wanting nothing."*
> *James 1:2-4*

The phrase **"My Brethren,'** is from the Greek word, **'Adelphos'** meaning, a brother; also designate a community of love based on the commonality of believers due to Christ's work (Matt 12:50; Mark 10:29-30; Acts 12:17.

The phrase **'count it all** joy' is from the Greek word, **'Chara'** meaning; to rejoice, joy or rejoicing, exultation, exuberant joy, good cheer, gladness of heart. This may not be how you feel concerning the particular text yet it is the attitude that will see you through!

The phrase 'when you fall into' 'is from the Greek word, **'Peripipto'** meaning to fall into; to be caught by)

The phrase, **'divers (various) temptations.'** is from the Greek word, **'Peirasmos'** meaning; testing. The meaning depends on who is doing the testing. When it is God, it is for the purpose of proving someone and never for the purpose of them falling.

The phrase **'Knowing this'** comes from the understanding that these test will come to fruition)

The phrase **that the trying' is from** the Greek word, **'Dokimion'** meaning; the means of proving; A test by which anything is proved or tried; for example; as faith is tested by afflictions) of your faith (your belief, confidence) will work patience."

The phrase**, 'But let patience'** is from the Greek word, **'Hupomone'** meaning, endurance as to things or circumstances and is associated with hope, and refers to the quality that does not surrender to circumstances or succumb under trial.

The phrase **'have her perfect'** is from the Greek word, **'Telelos' meaning; goal,** perfect (full) purpose; it is God's perfect (complete) work that brings perfect (complete) results. It is that which in part indicates the ultimate goal in or of heaven contrasted with something that can only have partial fulfillment on earth.

The word **'work'** is from the Greek word, **'Ergon'** meaning; generally denotes acts by which the man his genuineness and his faith. Faith is proven by its works; the works usually denotes comprehensively what a man is and how he acts.

The phrase, **'That ye may be perfect'** (growing in maturation) **and entire,** is from the Greek word, **'Holokleros'** from **'holos'** meaning; all, whole and **'kleros'** meaning; whole, having all its parts, sound, perfect; that which retains all which was allotted to it at the first, wanting nothing for its completeness; bodily, mental and moral entireness. It expresses the perfection of man before the fall. It also refers to one who has preserved, or who, having once lost has now regained his completeness!

The phrase, **'wanting nothing'** refers to; now having regained its completeness. Wanting nothing (for you are complete in Christ)! Everything has been made available for you to live a life of **Victory, through the Cross and what Jesus accomplished there!**

Most people like to stay within their comfort zone. However, there is little significant growth there. God created you with a purpose in mind a that purpose includes, **'your growth and maturity in Christ!'**

Why Testing?

Testing is designed to bring you and revelation concerning our relationship with God.

1. **Testing reveals your stability or lack thereof in faith!**

2. **Testing will reveal your (our) true attitude!**

3. **Testing is designed to strengthen you Spiritually, i.e. Caleb after 45 years was strong as ever, to take his mountain!**

4. **Testing brings change. It brings to light the changes necessary to reach higher heights in God!**

5. **Testing brings Growth and maturity!**

The Amplified Bible describes the result of testing, in what I believe to be the completeness of the believer.

"Consider it wholly joyful, my brethren, whenever you are enveloped in or encounter trials of any sort or fall into various temptations."

"Be assured and understand that the trial and proving of your faith bring out endurance and steadfastness and patience."

"But let endurance and steadfastness and patience have full play and do a thorough work, so that you may be [people] perfectly and fully developed [with no defects], lacing nothing." James 1:2-4 The Amplified Bible

Again, I believe that James in his letter describes not only how to face temptations (wholly joyful), but, also what the trials and temptations that every believer faces are for. He also reveals the results of going through trials and temptations; *"so that you may be [people] perfectly and fully developed [with no defects], lacking nothing."*

Paul speaks of the growth and maturity in, **'The Faith'** in the great book of Ephesians chapter 4. When the five-fold ministry (the Apostles; Prophets; Evangelists; Pastors and Teachers) are allowed to do their particular calling, the believer will be;

1. **Perfect:** (this is not perfection without fault or sin) but, it does mean to be separated (set apart) consecrated, and sanctified. As believers, we are to become separated from the world of sin, and separated unto God (Godliness). This growth and separation is revealed in detail in the great book of 2 Peter 1:12-8). This allows

the believer to be equipped the work of ministry and the edifying of the body of Christ (other believers).

2. <u>**To come into the knowledge of the Son of God (Jesus Christ);**</u> This is not referring to a head knowledge, but, to a knowledge that creates a personal relationship with Christ. It also refers to coming into the knowledge of the **'Cross and the Finished Work of Jesus Christ (what He accomplished there)!** In return, the believer can come into the measure and fullness of Jesus Christ. This is can only be accomplished though faith that has its object in the **'Cross and what Jesus Christ did there!'**

3. <u>**No longer being tossed about;**</u> This is referring to becoming steadfast and unmovable from **'The Faith!'** (Hebrews 10:23; 35-39). Not being tossed about is, referring to, the craftiness and sleight of men and the wind of every doctrine in which the **'Modern day Church'** has fallen.

4. <u>**Growing up into Him (Jesus Christ) in all things;**</u> This is referring to the maturation of the believer. (2 Peter 1:1-8; Jude 20)

<u>**As You Move Forward in Your Journey of Faith,**</u>
<u>**Count it All Joy, When you are facing Trials,**</u>
<u>**Tests and Temptation! You will Come out Victorious!**</u>
(1 John 5:4)

CHAPTER 2

The Origin of Trials, Tests and Temptations!

The trying of your faith comes from two very distinct places;

1. **God will put before the believer a test or trial.** It is important to understand, whatever test or trial God may send, it is never designed to make the believer fall into sin! We will examine some testing which are sent by God, in another chapter.

2. **Satan and his minions** will tempt the believer from every angle. Every temptation from the enemy (Satan) is always designed to remove the believer from their faith and obedience to the Word, resulting in sin!

Within this chapter we are going to discover how to navigate through the temptations that come from the enemy. First, let's examine the tools that the enemy will use in trying to remove the believer from his/hers faith.

*"But every man is tempted, when he is drawn
away of his own lust, and enticed." James 1:14*

The phrase, ***"But every man is tempted"*** presents the idea that no man is exempt from temptation. This began in the Garden of Eden when Adam fell. Adam gave birth to the sin nature that is alive within every living person. From that point forward there has never been a person who has not faced temptation in some manner.

The phrase, ***"when he is drawn away of his own lust and enticed."*** This statement clearly reveals the avenue in which Satan uses to in temptations. There is within every man the **'sin nature,'** and within that sin nature, lust resides.

The phrase, ***"drawn away,"*** is written in the present, passive, participle, meaning; a continuous or repeated action. However, it does not in itself indicate the time of the action. This also refers to the subject as receiving the action. To be drawn away presents the action taken to remove the believer from their faith.

The phrase, ***"of his own lust,"*** comes from the Greek word, ***'Epithumia'*** meaning; the active and individual desire, resulting from, ***'pathos,'*** meaning; the wound, hurt, to suffer. Thus, the diseased condition of the soul, from which various lusts spring. Again, this diseased condition of the soul was brought into existence through the disobedience of one fallen man, Adam. Even when a person is ***"born again,"*** the ***"sin nature"*** yet resides within the believer. However, the believer no longer has to walk under the dominion of the sin nature (Romans 6:14)

Within the sin nature there are three distinct areas the enemy (Satan), will use in temptation;

1. **<u>The lust of the flesh.</u>**

This refers to all the evil cravings which spring from the sin nature.

2. **<u>The lust of the eye.</u>**

This refers to the cravings from what we see, and the appeal that draws one into partaking, i. e. Eve. This kind of partaking results in the person falling into evil doings (sin).

3. **<u>The pride of life.</u>**

This refers to, one trusting in their own ability, power and resources. It leaves God out and desires to get ahead in life no matter the cost!

The word, ***"enticed,"*** is from the Greek word, ***'Deleazo,'*** meaning to catch by using bait, and is from the basis of being entrapped, fig. to delude, beguile, allure. This exactly defines the action of Eve (along with millions). Temptation begins by using the lust that resides within man. The sin nature along with its lust becomes the **'Bait,'** Satan uses to lure and entice men to sin.

It is interesting to note that Jesus Christ was tempted of Satan in these three areas, (Matthew 4:1-11). However, there was a vast difference in the way Christ was tempted. Jesus did not have a sin nature therefore; He did not have the lust of the flesh, the lust of the eye, nor the pride of life and was without any moral defect. Satan could not use (even though he tried), these three areas as bait to allure Jesus!

While the temptation with Christ was only external, with mankind, even the Godliest, it is both internal and external. As someone has said, temptation may come from within when a man *"is drawn away of his own lust,"* and it may come from without when he is *"enticed."* From within it is *"lust";* from without it is *"lure."* Jimmy Swaggart's Commentary of the book of James page 62 paragraph 3.

A great example is found in 2 Samuel 11 concerning King David. When he arose from his bed and began walking upon the roof of his house he noticed a woman (Bathsheba) washing herself. As David continued to watch her bathe, the lust within him became his own worst enemy. Her beauty began to *'lure'* him and it revealed his desire for a woman and the fulfillment of his sexual desires. While he was being tempted inwardly, the enticement and the drawing for his outward pleasure came into fulfillment. David not only committed adultery, he caused the murder of her husband, and it all began with a lust that resided within him.

<u>Combating Temptation</u>

Anyone that has faced any kind of temptation knows that at times it can be difficult to overcome. This is especially true when we try with the willpower within ourselves to combat what Satan throws at us. When we face the enemy with our willpower, it will produce failure!

It is a must to understand that we do not have the knowledge, wisdom, courage, strength and willpower within ourselves to combat Satan's devices. It takes an understanding and faith in the **'cross and what Jesus Christ accomplished** there. Having your faith on the right object and **'denying yourself'** while walking in the strength of Jesus Christ and the leading of the Holy Spirit, you then are in the right position to combat temptations!

> *"There hath no temptation taken you but such as is common to man: but God is faithful, who will not suffer you to be tempted above that ye are able; but with the temptation also make a way to escape, that you may be able to bear it."*
> *1 Corinthians 10:13*

As mentioned earlier, the way of escape is through the **"cross and the finished work of Jesus Christ."** Now, let's examine some things that will be necessary for the believer to walk in victory over temptations.

1. <u>Don't Give the Enemy Any Position of Opportunity!</u>

> *"Neither give place to the devil." Ephesians 4:27*

I really like the way the Amplified Bible reads;

> *"Leave no [such] room or foothold for the devil [give no opportunity to Him]*

Some temptations can be avoided by simply staying away from certain things that will bring temptation. Let me give a personal example;

In the middles sixties and early seventies I worked at RCA in Indianapolis, Indiana. Several of the guys would get together and go to lunch at a certain bar. Of course, I was right with them. Matter of fact, some of those guys had been drinking buddies. After giving my life back to Jesus Christ and beginning in the ministry (of course I had given up drinking any kind of alcohol (actually God delivered me) we were working overtime on a Saturday. When it came time for lunch I was walking with the guys and it dawned on me where they were going. I asked, and they said they were going to that favorite bar (they did have great sandwiches). I told them that I was not going. They tried to come up with all kinds of reasons why it would be okay for me to join them. One guy even went as far to say that he and his priest drink together (he was Catholic). My response was, ***"I'm not your priest and I am not going to put myself in a position to be tempted!"*** I knew at that time I had to stay away. I have to admit for a few years, beer was my favorite drink. Thank God for deliverance, I haven't touched any alcohol for over fifty years! Do not ever allow yourself to be put in a vulnerable position.

2. <u>Abstain from all appearance of evil.</u>

> ***"Abstain from evil {shrink from it and keep aloof from it] in whatever form or whatever kind it may be." 1 Thessalonians 5:22 the Amplified Bible***

The word, **'abstain'** is from the Greek word, **'Apechomai'** meaning, to keep oneself from, to abstain or refrain from. See Acts 15:20, 29

A great way to keep yourself from evil, is to ask yourself; ***"Is what I am about to do or partake of pleasing to God?"*** This within itself will help to avoid (abstain) from falling prey to the tactics of the devil.

3. <u>Keep Yourself Submitted to God.</u>

James in his Epistle gives great instruction concerning the believer and combating evil influences that are at war.

> *"Do ye think that the Scripture saith in vain, The Spirit that dwelleth in us lusteth to envy?"*

> *"But He (God) giveth more grace. Wherefore He saith, God resisteth the proud, but giveth grace unto the humble."*

> *"Submit yourselves therefore to God. Resist the devil and he will flee from you."*

> *"Draw nigh to God, and He will draw nigh to you. Cleanse your hands ye sinners; and purify your hearts, ye double minded." James 4: 5-8*

The above passage of scripture is filled with information that I believe is vital the believer to understand and apply to their every day faith walk!

In verse 5 James refers to several passages of scripture, however, I want you to notice the question being asked;

> *"Do you think that The Scripture saith in vain, The Spirit that dwelleth in us lusteth to envy?"*

The **'Spirit'** mentioned here is the Holy Spirit (contrary to some commentay's). The question is;

> *"Or do you suppose that the Scripture is speaking to no purpose that says, The Spirit Whom He has caused to dwell in us yearns over us and He yearns for the Spirit [to be welcome] with a jealous love?" [Jer. 3:14; Hos. 2:19} James 4:5 The Amplified Bible*

The Holy Spirit desires the latitude to work passionately, and earnestly, within the believer, with the purpose of leading and directing in his/her daily living (Romans 8). His leadership will direct the believer into the **'Newness of Life,'** and away from the **'Law of Sin and Death,'** which leads to destruction. See Romans chapters 6 and 8

It is with a sad heart to say, but most believers today do not know how to live a victorious life in Jesus Christ through the leading of the Holy Spirit. Most are being lead and directed by the fallen (sin) nature with victory ever eluding them.

Notice in verse 6;

> *"But He (God) giveth more grace (God's operational power. God operates through His grace). Wherefore He saith, God resisteth the proud but giveth grace unto the humble."*

> *"But He gives us more and more grace (power of the Holy Spirit, to meet this evil tendency and all others fully). That is why He says, God sets Himself against the proud and haughty, but*

gives grace [continually] to the lowly (those who are humble enough to receive it). [Proverbs 3:34]

We are going to talk in greater detail concerning the pride and haughty thinkers and the humble (those who live a life of humility) later in this chapter. So, let's focus on verses 7 and 8;

A. <u>Submit Yourself to God!</u>

The word **'Submit'** is from the Greek word, **'Hupotasso'** which is a compound word from, **'hupo,** meaning, under, and **'tasso'** meaning, to order. Together it means, to place in an orderly fashion under something. In this case it means submitting (continuously) to the plan that God has provided through the, **"Finished Work of Jesus Christ at Calvary1"** See Luke 9:23

B. <u>Resist the devil and he will flee from you!</u>

The phrase, *'resist the devil'* refers to the idea of casting him (the devil) aside and removing him from your presence. This can only be accomplished by walking in he liberty that Jesus Christ bought and paid for at Calvary! From that point, one must give themselves over to the direction and leading of the Holy Spirit in their everyday walk!

> *"There is therefore now no condemnation to them which are in Christ Jesus, who walk not after the flesh, but after the Spirit."*

> *"For the law of the Spirit of life in Christ Jesus hath made me free from the law of sin and death." Romans 8:1-2*

C. <u>Draw close to God!</u>

Notice, as the believer draws closer to God, He (God) in turn, draws closer to them. This can only happen by the believer having the correct object of their faith, which is faith in, **"The Cross and what Jesus Christ accomplished there.**

The phrase, **'Draw nigh to God,'** is from the Greek word, **'Eggizo,'** meaning, to bring near, to come near, approach. It is a verb and demands action on the part of the believer. When used in speaking of approaching God or coming near to God, it means communion with God in prayer and cherished fellowship with Him. (See Hebrews 7:19; James 4:8). The closer one comes to God, the greater the distance becomes from Satan. That certainly does not mean he (Satan) will not still try to attack and bring temptations. However, it does mean that you are closer to victory than defeat!

D. <u>Cleanse your hands ye sinners!</u>

The word, **'Cleanse'** is from the Greek word, **'Katharizo'** meaning; to cleanse from filth and become pure; to cleanse, in the sense of purification; also in the spiritual sense, to purify from pollution and the guilt of sin. This is dealing with walking in **'Sanctification'** which is a continuous action that takes place as the believer walks with the leading of the Holy Spirit, for He is the **'Spirit of Sanctification.'** Which means; He and He alone will direct the life of the believer into a life of separation from the world and a separation to God! Once again, this can only be accomplished when walking in faith and having its (faith) in the correct object, that being Jesus Christ and Him Crucified!

E. **Purify your hearts!**

This phrase is from the Greek word, **'Kardia'** in which the scriptures attribute to the heart, thoughts, mental reasoning, understanding, will, judgment, and affections. This is accomplished, when the believer allows his/her mind to be renewed on a daily basis and stop thinking like the world. (See Romans 12:1-2) With the renewing of the mind and walking in correct faith, it keeps the believer from being double minded and from conforming to the world. Remember, a double minded person is un-stable in all their ways. (See James 1:6-8).

The Apostle Peter in his first Epistle gives further instructions on how to combat the temptations coming from Satan and his minions;

> *"Therefore humble yourselves [demote, lower yourselves in your own estimation] under the mighty hand of God, that in due time He may exalt you."*

> *"Casting the whole of your cares [all your anxieties, all your worries, all your concerns, once and for all] on Him, for He cares for you affectionately and cares about you watchfully."*

> *"Be well balanced (temperate, sober of mind), be vigilant and cautious at all times; for that enemy of yours the devil, roams around [in fierce hunger], seeking someone to seize upon and devour." 1Peter 5:6-8 the Amplified Bible*

6. <u>Humble Yourself Under the Mighty Hand of God!</u>

The phrase, **'Humble yourselves'** in the original Greek text says, **'Be Humble or Suffer yourselves to be humbled.'**

The word, humble is translated *'lowly.'* Here, it is referring to separating yourself from a proud and haughty mindset and to be clothed with humility. The scripture declare that God resists the proud.

> *"Likewise, ye younger, submit yourselves unto the elder. Yea, all of you be subject one to another, and be clothed with humility: for God resisteth the proud, and giveth grace to the humble." 1 Peter 5:5*

The word , **'proud'** is from the Greek word, **'Huperephanos'** from *'huper'* meaning; over, and *'phainomai'* meaning; appear, Proud; one who shows himself above his fellow men, in honor preferring himself. (Luke 1:51). This can also refer to the overbearing, boastful arrogant individual. Notice; God resists such a one, meaning, that He is drawn away from and is set against such persons.

The Christian believer must be mentally in control. The idea is not only keep a renewed mind (Romans 12:2) but also to put on the mind of Christ. (Philippians 2:5-9; 4:8) The Christian believer must also **'pull down the strongholds which war against the mind and proud thinking;**

> *"For though we walk in the flesh, we do not war after the flesh:"*

"(For the weapons of our warfare are not carnal, but mighty through God to the pulling down of strongholds;)"

The Apostle Paul before he received the revelation of the **'Cross and what Jesus Christ did there,'** he spoke of a war that was within his mind.

***"But I see another law in my members,* (the law of sin and death desiring to use my physical body as an instrument of unrighteousness),** *warring against the Law of my mind* **(this is the Law of desire and willpower),** *and bringing me into captivity to the Law of sin* **(the Law of sin and death)** *which is in members* **(which will function through my members, and me make a slave to the Law of sin and death; this will happen to the most consecrated Christian if the Christian doesn't constantly exercise Faith in Christ and the Cross, understanding that it is through the Cross that all powers of darkness were defeated [Col. 2:14-15] This passage scripture was taken from, The Expositor's Study Bible, Jimmy Swaggart**

The phrase, *'I see another law'* the word **'another'** is from the Greek word, **'Heterozugeo'** from, **'heteros'** meaning, another, different, and from, **'zugos'** meaning a yoke; to draw the other side of a different yoke, meaning; different from each other.

The word, **'warring'** is from the Greek word, (Fig.) to attack (by impl.) to destroy, to war against. This word means to make a military expedition, to take the field (in this case, the mind), against anyone, to oppose, to war against.

The phrase, **'against the Law of my mind'** this is the Law of desire and willpower. Satan attacks the believer by using the **'sin nature'** that dwells within to break down their willpower and desire to do what is good.

The phrase, **'and brining me into captivity'** refers to the Law of Sin and Death (see Romans 8:2) which results in a life of continuous sin and which leads to death.

Paul went on to say;

> *"O wretched man that I am! Who shall deliver me from the body (this body) of death?"*

> *"I thank God through Jesus Christ our Lord. So then with the mind I myself serve the Law of God; but with the flesh the law of sin." Romans 7:24-25*

The phrase, **'with the mind'** is from the Greek word, **'Nous'** meaning; the organ of mental perception and apprehension; the organ of conscious life; To perceive with the mind, as distinct from perception by feeling. It is within the mind that the enemy wars and brings a perception contrary to the Word of God. This is one reason why the believer is admonished to renew their mind on a daily basis. Romans 12:2

The following scripture says it a lot better than I ever could.

> *"For I say, through the grace given unto me, to every man that is among you, not to think of himself more highly than he ought to think, but to think soberly (being mentally stable) according*

> *as God hath dealt to every man the measure of*
> *faith." Romans 12:3*

I have often said; **"Don't think you are all of that *and* a bag of chips!"**

Dwell on that for awhile and you will get it! A person can get themselves in a lot of trouble by allowing pride to rise up within them. God hates a proud (high haughty) minded look! **See Proverbs 6:17**

> *"Casting down (pull down and throwing away)*
> *imaginations (arguments, wrong reasonings,*
> *wrong conclusions), and every high thing that*
> *exalteth itself against the knowledge of God,*
> *and bringing into captivity every thought to the*
> *obedience of Christ;" 2 Cor. 10:3-5; Emphasis*
> *are mine*

The phrase, **'against the knowledge of God,'** is from the Greek word, **'Gnosis'** meaning knowledge, from **'ginosko,' to know experientially.** This is a present and fragmentary knowledge as contrast with, **'epignosis'** which is a clear and exact knowledge which expresses a more thorough participation on the part of the subject.

Do not allow the enemy to shadow nor take away what you are experiencing in your walk of faith in Christ Jesus and the Cross!

The phrase **'every thought,'** is from the Greek word, **'Noema;'** from **'noeo'** meaning, to perceive; to have a thought or concept of the mind (2 Cor. 10:5); a device, contrivance (2 Cor. 2:11) the understanding, the mind (2 Cor. 3:14; 4:4; 11:3; Phil. 4:7).

The phrase **'to the obedience of Christ'** is from the Greek word, **'Hupakeo;'** from **'hupakouo'** meaning; to obey, listen to something, hearken. It refers to subjection to the saving will of God revealed in Christ and referred to as obedience to the truth (1 Peter 1:22)

The enemy (Satan and his minions) are working trying to keep the believer from knowing and understand the **'Cross and what Jesus Christ did there.' For it is in the Cross and the finished work of Jesus Christ that victory was won and given to the believer. Our mind and thinking and faith must be focused on what Jesus Christ has accomplished at the Cross! (1 Cor. 1:17-18; Hebrews 12:1-2)**

5. <u>Cast 'ALL' your cares upon Christ Jesus.</u>

> *"Casting the whole of your care [all your anxieties, all your worries, all your concerns, once and for all] on Him, for He cares for you affectionately and cares about you watchfully. 1 Peter 5:7 Amplified Bible see also [Psalm 55:22]*

There are so many passages of scripture that reveals just how much Jesus Christ cares and how watchful over the believer He is. One particular passage is when the disciples were in a boat and in the midst of a storm. Jesus saw how the disciples were struggling (toiling) and He went to them on the water. (Mark 6:45-52)

Jesus Christ is watching and looking after you no matter where you may be and no matter your condition. He is there saying, *"Don't worry nor fret for I have got this!" (Psalm 37:1-7)*

6. <u>Be sober;</u>

Being sober is to be in mental control. As mentioned previously, the believer must renew their mind.

> *"And be not conformed the to this world: but be ye transformed by the renewing of your mind, that ye may prove what is that good, and acceptable, and perfect will of God." Romans 12:2*

The phrase, *"And be not conformed to this world,'* the word, *'conformed'* is from the Greek word, *'Suschematizo'* this is a compound word coming from, **'sun'** meaning together with, and, *'schematize'* meaning, to fashion, which is from *'schema.'* Together, they take on the idea of not being fashion with this age i.e. world. Do not fall in with the external and fleeting fashions of this age, i.e. world, nor be fashioned to them, but undergo a deep inner change by the qualitative renewing of your mind.

The phrase, *"be ye transformed"* is from the Greek word, *'Metamorphoo'* from, *'meta'* denoting change of condition, and *'morphoo'* the idea of transformation refers to an invisible process in Christians which takes place or begins to take place already during their life in this age. It also comes with the idea to renovate (make) a person different for a qualitative new use. We get the word **'metamorphosis'** which speaks of a change. However, this change is on the outside while **'metamorpoo'** beings on the inside of a person.

The phrase, *"by the renewing of your mind"* the word *'renewing'* is from the Greek word *'Anakainosis'* related to a qualitatively new use. This is a renewing and or the renovation which makes a person different than in the past, to renew qualitatively.

The phrase, *'of your mind'* is from the Greek word, *'Nous'* meaning; the mind, the organ of mental perception and apprehension.

To be *'sober'* is to be in your right mind which is being renewed daily. This brings the idea of not fashioning your thinking like the world. At the time of this writing we are facing a pandemic of **'Co-vid 9 virus.'** When it was first announced, I was amazed at the Christians who immediately allowed the spirit of fear to take control. Many have remained d in fear and it has spread; like wildfire. The believer of today needs to be reminded of two important things; **1. This kind of fear is a spirit. 2. God did not give you and I that spirit. He did give the believer;**

> *"God did hath not given us the spirit of fear;*
> *but of power, and of love, and of a sound mind."*
> *2 Tim. 1:7*

It is time to walk in the soundness of the mind that Jesus Christ has provided through the Cross!

7. Be Vigilant;

This comes with the idea of being alert, awake and watchful at all times. It also refers to being aware of your surroundings. Without this watchfulness and alertness one can be blindsided and overthrown by the enemy! Your (the believer) victory is making the object of your faith in the **'Cross and the Finished Work of Jesus Christ!'** (John 19:30) We will discuss this in greater detail in another chapter.

Being vigilant is being alert, being watchful and awake, at all times It is extremely important that the believer be aware of his/her surroundings. We must guard against having tunnel vision! Remember, there is an enemy who is like a roaring lion who is wanting to devour the **'Child of God!'**

The believer is under attack continuously by the enemy, who is trying to remove them from their **'Faith in the Cross and what Jesus Christ accomplished there!'** It is important for the believer to become steadfast in **'The Faith!'**

8. Put on The Whole Armor of God. (Ephesians 6:11-17)

When reading this great passage of scripture, I want you to notice the phrase, *"the whole armor."* In order to defeat the enemy (Satan and his minions) you cannot pick and choose what part of the armor you want to put on. It must be all of the armor that God has supplied. This armor has been proven and it will stand the test **(Isaiah 59:16-17).**

 The believer, above all, must take up the **'Shield of Faith,'** so all the fiery darts that Satan throws can be quenched (stopped). That is the proper **'Shield of Faith!' Once again, 'the Shield of Faith' is a correct faith, which has its object, "the Cross and the finished work of Jesus Christ!**

9. Continue to Speak The Word.

When Israel was getting prepared to take the land of Promise, God instructed Joshua to keep the Word in his mouth (Joshua 1:8) The reason being, words are powerful, and by our speech we can walk in the promises of God , or, we can talk ourselves out of what God has promised.

It is speaking of doubt and unbelief that kept an entire generation to miss out of what God promised (Numbers 13:28-33 It also reveals the power of our speaking.

There is within every believer the ability to speak life or death (Proverbs18:21) The speaking of the Word can (will) bring healing and deliverance (Matthew 8:5-10. Jesus spoke the Word when being tempted by the devil (Matthew 4:1-11. Jesus also taught that we are justified or condemned by the words that proceed from our mouth (Matthew 12:37). Mark 11:22-24

10. <u>Remain Steadfast in The Faith. Hebrews 10:23-25;</u>

To be steadfast in the faith, and this is not just any kind of faith, but it is (and I realize I sound like a broken record, but, this is beneficial to you) **'Faith in the Cross and what Jesus Christ accomplished there!'**

<u>REMEMBER!</u>

The believer is under attack continuously by the enemy, who is trying to remove them from their **'Faith in the Cross and what Jesus Christ accomplished there!'** It is important for the believer to become steadfast in **'The Faith!'**

CHAPTER 3

Common Mistakes Made By Believers when Being Tried and Tested! Part 1

"Beloved, think it not strange concerning the firery trial which is to try you as though some strange thing happened unto you." 1 Peter 4:12

Apostle Peter wrote this great letter to give encouragement to the believers who were under great persecution. He admonished them to stand and endure the trying of their faith. He was also preparing them for even greater trials that were ahead of them. The first empire-wide persecution of the Christians believers took place in about 249 A.D. under the tyrant emperor Decius. He was known by Christians as **'the fierce tyrant.'** There were hundreds if not thousands of Christian persecuted and put to death during his reign. However, in the second year of his reign, **'the ferocity of the** [anti-Christian] persecution had eased off, and the earlier tradition of tolerance had begun to assert itself. Despite no indication in surviving texts that the edict targeted any particular group, Christians bore the brunt of the persecution and never forgot the reign of Decius.

In other areas persecution became very intense. One such place in the early second century was in Bilthynia, which was one of the provinces to which the Apostle Peter addressed. The call went out to not only save those Christian believers if they would deny their faith.

The Christian of believer today may not be as great as then, this is especially true in North America however, there is a spiritual onslaught against all who dare believe and have their faith in the **'Cross and the Finished Work of Jesus Christ.'**

At the time of this writing (late 2020) the believing Christian (those who Stand and proclaim Jesus Christ as Lord and Savior) could possibly be facing some of our greatest trial in **'The United States of America.'** We (the Christian) are engaged in a warfare now that I not seen before. Satan is working overtime trying to stop and destroy the Church. We know beyond any doubt that he will not succeed (Matt. 16:13-19). My concern is for those that will give into the deception and deceit that is in the world today. **'EVERY CHRISTAIN MUST CONTINUE TO STANDFAST IN THEIR (OUR) FAITH IN CHRIST AND WHAT HE DID AT CALVARY!'**

The trials and tests that we (the believer) are facing today may not consist of being boiled in oil, thrown into a fiery furnace or a lions-den. We may not be facing being beheaded as is done is some countries however it is still an intense spiritual warfare.

Understanding Trials and Tests!

As believers, we may not understand why we must face being tried and tested. We may even wonder why God permits such things to happen. It may have even crossed our minds, **'where is God's divine protection?'** As long as we remain here on earth attacks and trials will remain a part of our everyday living. **Remember, untested faith, is a faith that cannot be trusted!** Without a proper understanding of the cross and what Jesus Christ did there it becomes very difficult if not impossible to live a life of victory. Without that knowledge it can be difficult to be a genuine believer and follower of Jesus Christ in today's world. Jesus said;

> *"In this world ye shall have tribulation (this represents an action that was completed in the past yet it has continuing results) but be of good cheer (this comes as a command to do something and it involves a continuing and repeated action) I have overcome the world." John 16:33*

There is little doubt that trials and tests will come our way. The question is, **'why, and what is the purpose?'** These questions are something that we will endeavor to answer.

1. **Trails and Tests measure how strong your (our) faith is and how strong (stable) we are in the faith** One measuring tool is to discover what the believer is willing to give up (change) for the moving forward of the kingdom of God.

2. **Trials reveal your (our) strengths and weaknesses.** When the believers back is against the wall and attacks are coming against their faithful stand in Christ how strong or how weak the believer is will be revealed.

3. **Trials and tests can be a teacher.** Being tried and tested can be a schoolmaster which teaches the believer to trust God and become more faithful. This can be a time that draws the believer closer to God (James 4:7-10). Trials and tests can also be a teaching tool for the believer to depend solely on the **'Cross and what Jesus Christ did there.'**

4. **Trials and testing will reveal the ability to show patience and endurance.** How can the believer know the extent of endurance and patience without being tested? The answer is, **'they can't!** I can remember running cross country in high school. We would run two miles, while running I would save enough energy for the final kick. There was one guy who would always out run me (he was a senior and I was a sophomore). I learned a lot about patience and endurance by just wanting to catch him, which I never did, however, I came close a time or two. Whether we like it or not, being tried and tested is a necessity for spiritual growth.

5. **Being tried and tested can be a great testimony (witness) to others.** The way the believer faces (goes through) testing and trials can be a drawing tool for un-believers to come to Christ. When our faith in Jesus Christ is put on display it will not go unnoticed. When others see you (the believer) living in hope and

remaining faithful during tough times, it will get the attention of those around you. This can be a great opportunity for the Holy Spirit to speak to the hearts of others and draw others to Christ.

Living and walking close to Jesus Christ will draw persecution and trials. One great man by the name of John Wesley describes it this way;

'He was riding on his horse along a road one day when it dawned on him that three whole days had passed in which he had suffered no persecution. Not a brick or an egg had been thrown at him for three days.'

'Alarmed, he stopped his horse, and exclaimed, "Can it be that I have sinned, and am backslidden?"

'Slipping from his horse, Wesley went down on his knees and began interceding with God to show him where, if any, there had been a fault.'

'A rough fellow on the other side of the hedge, hearing the prayer, looked across and recognized the preacher. "I'll fix that Methodist preacher, he said" Picking up a brick and tossing it over at him, it missed its, and fell harmlessly beside John. Whereupon Wesley leaped to his feet joyfully exclaiming, "Thank God, it's all right. I still have his presence."

If only the believers of today had the mind set and tenacity of John Wesley, only God knows what we (the believers) could get done!

6. **The Character of the Believer is being Tried, and Tested.** When being in the midst of a trial and or test it becomes examination time. This is a vital part of teaching and receiving revelation of just who we are! When facing a crisis, it can become a productive disclosure of one's self. When in the middle of a fiery trial, this is a great opportunity to find the fullness of strength and resources that are available There may be times when you may think you cannot, it, that is a time to take hold of the Word of God and allow it to bring forth victory in you and about you!

7. **Hard Trials and Tests makes for Endurance (as we mentioned earlier) to run this race.**

   "Wherefore we are also compassed about with so great a cloud of witnesses, let us lay aside every weight, and the sin which doth so easily beset us, and let us run with patience the race that is set before us." Hebrews 12:1

   The word, *'witnesses'* in this passage of scripture is extremely important to understand. It has been (and still is) taught, that this refers to the Saints of the Old Testament Saints looking down on us and watching the believer running the race. However, that teaching is incorrect. It is goes far deeper than the Old Testament. The word, *'witnesses'* is from the Greek word, *'martus'* meaning; one who testifies, or can testify, to what he/ she has seen and heard or know by any other means. This defines those who have proved that their faith in the, **'Cross and the Finished Work of Jesus Christ'** is strong and genuine.

8. **Trials and testing not only reveal a tough, hardened character, they also develop and, birth the hidden beauty within the believer.** The Apostle Paul instructed Timothy to; ***"Endure hardness as a good soldier."*** ***2 Timothy 2:3.*** As I have said before, going through tough trials, tests and hard places brings forth the true character and nature of Jesus Christ within the believer. Notice the following;

    'The strength of every soul is less
    Till it has touched the wilderness,
    And learned to be alone;
    Tis from the desert we command
    The prospect of our promised land
    And sight of Judah's throne
    Tis in the desert God prepares
    His destined ones to be heirs
    Of ages yet to be;
    For only they who stand and wait
    Beside the shade of suffering's, though late,
    To bid the bond free!

    Author unknown

No matter the severity of your trial and test that you may be facing, you can make it through with victory! Keep in mind a statement that I heard years ago and I have used it often; **"Tough Times Never Last, But Tough People Do!**

The legendary coach John Wooden (who in my opinion was one of the greatest basketball coaches) said;

"Things work out the best for people, who make the best of the way things work out!"

YOU TOO, CAN MAKE THE BEST OUT OF WHATEVER YOU ARE FACING! JUST HANG TOUGH AND KEEP THE (YOUR) FAITH IN THE CROSS AND THE FINISHED WORK OF JESUS CHRIST!

CHAPTER 4

Common Misunderstanding When Being Tested and Tried! Part 2

'Thinking'
(My Trials and Tests are Uncommon)

"There hath no temptation taken you but such is common to : man: but God is faithful, who will not suffer you to be tempted above that ye are able; but with the temptation also make a way to escape that ye may be able to bear it."
1 Cor. 10:13

The scriptures throughout the entirety of the Bible bear witness regarding trials and testing. It can be difficult to understand that being tested and tried is for our good (Ro. 8:28) whether the test is sent by God or that He permits the trying of our faith. One of the main factors in facing trials and tests is the development of Christian character, i.e. **'Becoming Christ Like!'**

Standing through the trails and tests in your life can bring great rewards. It may seem impossible to come out in victory while going through them. However, if you stand firm in **'the faith,'** you will ultimately come out with victory and have a greater understanding of seeing God's hand at work. Please, understand, I am not saying that God causes the turmoil or tragedy that is in this world, what I am saying is, God will take every opportunity to deliver blessings and victory in some form or fashion.!

The world is full of people who are embittered by what they are facing i.e. going through. Their character may change while facing their particular affliction. I have seen people who naturally were mild mad their mannered until a storm of various afflictions comes an their entire attitude change. It can be difficult to understand the true meaning of what we face in life. It can also become difficult to rely on God's great grace to see you through. It can also be difficult to recognize the hand of God working within these adverse circumstances, while not understanding that God will seem them through (Psalm 34:19)!

We all face adverse circumstances and situations that cause questions to rise. The greater questions are, **'Why all of this is happening to me?' 'What did I do to cause all of this?'** These, along with many other questions we are going to try to answer within the following pages.

Let's examine the following scripture to help clear up some misunderstanding and mistakes concerning the trials and tests we face.

"There hath no temptation taken you but such is common to man: but God is faithful, who will not suffer you to be tempted above that ye are able; but with the temptation also make a way to escape that ye may be able to bear it." 1 Cor. 10:13

1. **Thinking the trial or tests you are facing is unusual and uncommon.** I have witnessed so many people who think that their particular situation is unusual and not like anything anybody has ever faced. Even if they do realize that it is not unusual, they think that their situation is greater and more painful than what anyone has ever gone through or felt. The Apostle Paul makes it very clear that the believer will be faced with trials and temptations and that they (the believer) are not the first to face whatever is before them.

The phrase, *'There hath no temptation (trial or test) taken you'* reveals the certainty we all will face trials and testing. It is impossible for the Christian to grow and mature spiritually without facing difficulties in life. **Victory only comes by winning battles!**

The phrase, *'but such as is common to man'* the word *'common'* is from the Greek word, *'anthropinos'* meaning; after the manner of man. This also reveals the limitation that God has placed upon Satan. He can only do what God allows Him to do. God is the one who draws the line and places restrictions on him. (Job 1:1-13) The Amplified Bible speaks concerning this phrase as;

> ***"For (no trial regarded as enticing   to   sin,
> no matter how it comes or where it leads)
> has overtaken you and laid hold on you that
> is not common to man [that is, no temptation
> or trial has come to you that is beyond human
> resistance and that is not adjusted and adapted
> and belonging to human experience, and such
> as man can bear}.***

2. **Thinking that trials and tests are unexpected.** The above passage of scripture reveals that trails and tests are inevitable. However, let me clarify something; I am in no way suggesting that something bad is awaiting you and I around every corner. However, as stated before, the scriptures are clear that no one is exempt from facing trails and tests in life. With that being said, a trial or test should not come as a surprise. As believers, we know that Satan comes to steal, kill, and destroy while Jesus Christ came to give life and that more abundantly (John 10:10). A lot of the confusion about trials and tests is, where they are coming from. Remember, God never designs a trail or test that solicits evil, that is what Satan does!

Think of the many things that the Apostle Paul faced during his ministry (2 Cor. 11:24-33). Along with Paul consider the many tests that great men and women who went before us faced. God does allow trials and tests, however, they are all for our benefit. Often times, if not every time, the believer faces a test that reveals where we are in **'the faith!** So, never let your guard down and get blind-sided by the tests in your life!

3. **Thinking that what you are going through is the result of sin.** So often the believer can fall into the trap that the test or trial they are facing is due to sin in their life. Jesus was asked this very question concerning a blind man;

"And as Jesus passed by, He saw a man which was blind from his birth."

"And His disciples asked Him, saying, Master, who did sin, this man, or his parents, that he was born blind?"

"Then Jesus answered, Neither, hath this man sinned, nor his parents: but that the works of God should be manifest in him."

I can remember many years ago, I was in the Hospital facing my second back surgery. The pain I was in was almost unbearable. The doctor had tried several things in trying to avoid surgery. I'll never forget, a preacher came to see me. While sitting on the edge of my bed (why do people do that when you are in so much pain? I'll never know!) he proceeded to tell me that I was in that condition due to sin in my life. My response was; **"No, that is not true. I am here facing this because I did not take proper care of my body!"** Please, understand that being in sin can and does create some bad situations and results. That is not the context in which we are looking at considering being tried and tested. I have said it before, and I will say it again, Satan is the one who puts a test or trial before the believer in trying to solicit evil. Whereas, God, never sends a trial or test that creates sin. It is important to distinguish the origin of what you are facing!

Saint Francis de Sales admirably put it this way (when dealing with temptations to sin or otherwise). ***"A dog goes on barking because he is not let in, and when the door is opened, and he is allowed to enter, he ceases barking. So, the persistence of a trail is generally a sign that we have not yielded, that we have kept the door of our heart fast closed against trials. When yielded, the trial generally ceases for a while!*** Well said!

4. **Becoming Over Anxious to Rid Yourself of the Trial, Test, or Temptation.** As one writer observed, he saw raw material out of which our crown of glory is to be made fashionable. However, the trail and or test is intended by God to do a certain work in developing our soul and spirit. Trying to remove or get away from a trail or test prematurely can and will damage the growing process. Let me share a personal experience. When I was about six years old, we lived on a farm. Under one of our buildings a duck was nesting. When I got off of the school bus I would run and check on the nest that was full of eggs. One day, when I went to check on the nest, some of the eggs were cracking and even moving some. So, I had this bright idea of helping them to come into this world. So, I began peeling the shell so they could get out. After helping those little ducklings to come into the world, they all died. I felt terrible for what I did. When I told my grandpa what I did, after giving me a stern lecture, he told me how the struggle of those little ducklings to get out of the egg shell would strengthen them to live.

You may be thinking: "**What am I supposed to do when facing that extreme tests?**" The Apostle Paul found himself in this very situation asking the same kind of question.

> *And lest I should be exalted above measure through the abundance of the revelations, there was given to a thorn in the flesh, the messenger of Satan to buffet me, lest I should be exalted above measure."*
>
> *"For this thing I besought the Lord thrice, that is might be removed." 2 Cor. 12:7-8*

I realize that there are many questions about the thorn in Paul's flesh as to what it was. However, I want to focus on Paul's request to remove it from him, and the response of God. Like anyone, Paul, was certainly anxious to get rid of what this thorn. Notice God's answer;

> *"And He (God) said unto me, My Grace is sufficient for thee: for my strength is made perfect in weakness. Most gladly therefore will I rather glory in my infirmities, that the power of Christ may rest upon me."*
>
> *Therefore I take pleasure in infirmities, in reproaches, in necessities, in persecutions, in distresses for Christ sake: for when I am weak, then am I strong." 2 Cor. 12:9-10*

I am convinced upon the Apostle Paul receiving an understanding of the **'Cross and the Finished Work (what He accomplished) of Jesus Christ'** that he was able to have a different perception of his life and what God wanting to accomplish through him In other words, we must allow the Holy Spirit the latitude to work in us so He can work through us!

Think of a test being the invisible finger or hand of God striking a hidden cord in your life for His purpose. Think on the following;

    A. Trials reveal the very best in us! Phil. 3:21

    B. Trials can cause a greater consecration and deeper devotion and service to God!

    C. Trials can be sinking shaft which strikes a deeper vein that out the gold in us! Phil. 2:13

    D. That trails consist of the Angels of God in disguise sent to minister to you!

    E. Trials can make life in Christ sweeter!

The problem of getting anxious (to remove ourselves from a trial or test) can result in disaster. It is important to wait upon God and allow the Holy Spirit the latitude to do a work in us. (Romans 8). Also, we are to be anxious for nothing and to only seek the enabling power of God's great grace!

    5. <u>Thinking that the trial or test is greater than you can bear.!</u>

This type of thinking can result in discouragement and despair. The Apostle Paul gave great encouragement to the Church in Cornith concerning this matter. Going back to our original passage of scripture lest take a deeper look into this type of thinking;

> *"There hath no temptation taken you but such is
> common to : man: but God is faithful, who will
> not suffer you to be tempted above that ye are
> able; but with the temptation also make a way to
> escape that ye may be able to bear it." 1 Cor.13*

I like the way the Amplified reads concerning this subject;

> *"But God is faithful [to His Word and to His
> compassionate nature]. And He [can be trusted].
> Not to let you be tempted and tried and assayed
> beyond your ability and strength of resistance
> and power to endure.*

If you are facing a trial or test and it has seemingly grown heavy or overbearing, it is because you are looking in the wrong places and at the wrong thing. It is when we put our faith exclusively in the **'Cross and what Jesus Christ accomplished there!** What we are facing (bearing) will become lighter and you will be able to see light at the end of the tunnel!

There is not trial or test that you will ever face that you will not have the ability through the Holy Ghost to endure. You can, and will make it!

There is a beautiful passage by At. Ephrem Syrus, where he likens the soul under temptation yet in God's hands, to the vessels which a potter makes. They are made of clay, in itself poor material, and quite useless until it has passed through the furnace and been hardened by exposure to its heat. The potter watches the vessel in the furnace and tempers the heat with great judgment, so that it may exactly affect its purpose. To little heat, and the vessels would not properly harden; to much heat, and they would be cracked and ruined. Then the potter regulates not only the heat of the furnace, but the time during which the pots are exposed to its operation. If he withdraws them too soon, they would still be soft and useless; if he left them in too long, they would become broken and spoiled. So, says St. Ephrem.

It is evident that God is the potter and we are the clay (Isa 64:8; Jer. 18:2-6) Therefore, God deals with us, and out of vessels of human clay makes the saints of heaven. And the process is the same; human clay has to pass through the furnace of trials and temptations are, so to speak, graduated precisely to each one's ability to bear. A/G. Mortimer; see also Romans 8:28. God is in t he middle of your particular situation (trail or test) working out good for you. With that in mind, it certainly makes easier to go through to **'Victory!**

Thank of it this way; Thank God I am not what I used to be, however, I am not yet what I am going to be, **'God is still working on me!**

<u>Not Understanding God's provision of escape!</u>

The last part of this great passage of scripture that we are studying here reads;

> ***"but will with the temptation also make a way of escape, that you my be able to bear it"***

Every believer faces some kind of temptation or test, however, we may not face the same kind of temptation. However, whatever trial or test you are facing, God has made a way *"of escape!*

First, it is important to understand that God has put limitations on Satan concerning what he can and cannot do. Remember, when Satan comes at the believer with a temptation (the original word is test or testing) it is always to solicit evil.

Secondly, as we have mentioned before, while God does send the believer through a trial and or test, it is never to do evil. I have often heard it said many times that when God is testing the believer it is so God will see where the believer stands in their faith. Since God is omniscient (all knowing), that statement cannot be the case. When God sends a trial or test it is for the benefit of the believer. The test is to reveal to the believer any and all changes necessary for growth and maturity.

The phrase, *"make a way"* in the original writings was, *"the way"* meaning a special way, which is referring to only **'one way!'** Some may resort to fasting and a deeper prayer life, while some may spend more time in the Word. While all of these are great and something every believer should partake in, these are not **'the way'** that the Apostle Paul was speaking of.

Jesus said;

> *"Jesus saith unto him (Thomas), I am the way, the truth, and the life: no man cometh unto the Father but by me. John 14:6*

The phrase, *" I am the way"* is from the Greek word, *'Hodos'* meaning; way, path; a way, a road in which one travels; a way, manner of life or action, custom; particularly, following, a way leading to a method or manner of obtaining. When Jesus said, *"I am the way,"* and no one comes to the Father in an established state of blessedness but only through Christ. This is derived from the Greek word, *'methodeia'* meaning the method of following or pursuing of orderly and technical procedures in the handling of a subject.

The phrase, *"the truth"* is from the Greek word, *'Alethela'* meaning; truth, as unveiled reality lying at the basis of and agreeing with an appearance; the manifested, or the veritable essence of matter The reality pertaining to an appearance. There are also three distinctive meanings;

1. **The Truth; which is opposite to falsehood, error or insincerity.**

2. **The Truth; as being opposite to types, emblems, or shadows.**

3. **Integrity, rectitude of nature.**

These definitions reveal Jesus Christ as **'the truth!'** There is simply no other truth!

The phrase, *"the life"* is from the Greek word, *'Zoe'* meaning; life, referring to the principle of life in the Spirit and Soul.

It is very clear that Jesus Christ is' not only **'The Way'** but the only **'Way!'** With this being said, **'the way of escape (going through trails and tests) is through 'Faith in the Cross and the finished work of Jesus Christ!' (1 Cor. 1:17-18)**

Keep in mind, no matter the intensity of the temptations, trials and tests, Jesus Christ paid the price for **'YOUR VICTORY!** To understand the totality of His provisions for victory and walking in the **'Newness of Life,'** Study the following chapters of scriptures (which are my favorites) and allow the Holy Spirit to bring the illumination and revelation that they contain. **Romans chapters 5, 6, 7, and 8. I challenge you to read and study these four chapters along with Romans chapter 8 and I guarantee your life will change for the better!**

CHAPTER 5

Faith Tried By Fire

Thee trials and tests the early church faced were certainly of fire. You may have seen clips or pictures of the early Christians being tried by fire. What I mean by the phrase, **'tried by fire,'** I am not limiting the early Christian being tried by a literal fire. I am talking about the intensity of what those in the faith faced. Some were fed to lions, some burned at the stake, some had boiling lead poured upon them and theses all died a miserable, torturing death. Some were branded with hot irons placed on the private parts, while others were soaked in flammable cloth and set on fire. Some were tortured by having their limbs ripped from their bodies while, others were beheaded. The list is continuous with many different methods of torture being placed upon the believers. **See Hebrews 11:36-40**

When everything is put into the right perspective, it makes what you and I are facing today, in the United States of America small. I am certainly not minimizing what we (the believers) face today. However, it is a different time and a different day, with the believers facing some kind of persecution or test. The end results, should be, one of victory. We are going to reveal the key (methods) in facing every trial, temptation, and test.

As we get started in this part of our study on **'Your Faith being Tried by Fire!'** It is important to realize once again, God will never send you (the believer) through a trial or test which creates evil. Those types of trying and tempting come from the evil one himself, Satan. Keep this in mind, as we have been examining the great differences between how one's faith is tried.

When thinking of faith being tried by fire, most often, the first thing that comes to mind is the three Hebrew boys (Shadrach, Meshach, and Abed-nego); being thrown into Nebuchadnezzar fiery furnace.

Nebuchadnezzar was made aware of certain Jews (mainly, Shadrach, Meshach and Abed-nego), who refused to bow, kneel and worship the gods of Babylon and the golden image that the king had set up.

When approached by the King asking them, ***"do you not serve my gods, nor worship the golden image which I have set up?' (Daniel 3:14)***

The question, **'Is it true?'** is one that each of us must give an answer to. **'Who are we bowing to and worshipping?'**

The king continued to ask, **'Who is the God that shall deliver you out of my hand and from the fiery furnace?'** They responded saying, **'we are not careful to answer you in this matter.' (*"We are not careful to answer you in this matter,"*** *is somewhat clumsy in the English translation. It actually means that it is not something they have to think about or give careful consideration to, as the matter is not open for discussion. It is a decision they made a long time ago, and the consequences are of no concern.) Jimmy Swarragrt The Expositor's Study Bible*

> *"If it be so, our God Whom we serve is able to deliver us from the burning fiery furnace, and He will deliver us out of your hand, O king."*
>
> *"But if not, be it known unto you, O king, that we will not serve your gods, nor worship the golden image which you have set up." Daniel 3:17-18*

Nebuchadnezzar became so infuriated with their answer, so he demanded the furnace to be heated seven times hotter than ever before. Why seven times hotter? The Babylonians worship seven planets each one having its own god who would send decrees. (An, Enlil, Enki, Nin Hursag, Nanna, Utu and Inanna along with Marduk which was their national god). It could be possible the reason behind the fire being seven times hotter was to appease these gods.

It is possible that the furnace was set up as some kind of kiln with openings at the top and bottom to allow easier access to keep the flames burning. There is a book called *"The Song of the Three Hebrew Children,"* that reveals their stance against Nebuchadnezzar.

Nebuchadnezzar commanded the mighty men in his army to bind (they were bound in their coats, their hosen and their hats, Along with their other garments) Shadrach, Meshach and Abed-nego and throw them into the fiery furnace. The furnace was so hot and the flames leaping so high that it killed the men who through them in the furnace.

> *"Then Nebuchadnezzar the king was astonied (terrified), and rose up in haste, and spoke, and said unto his counselors, Did not we cast three men bound into the midst of the fire? They answered and said unto the king, True, O king,"*

> *"He answered and said, Lo, I see four men loose, walking in the midst of the fire, and they have no hurt; and the form of the fourth is like the Son of God." Daniel 3:23-24*

The phrase, **'The Son of God,'** originally was written as, **'a son of God.'**

> *"And the princes, governors, and captains, and the king's counselors, being gathered together, saw these three men, upon whose bodies the fire had no power, nor was an hair of their head singed, neither were their coats changed, nor the smell of fire had passed on them." Daniel 3:27*

Nebuchadnezzar declared, *"The God of Shadrach, Meshach and Abed-nego, Who has sent His Angel and delivered His servants who trusted Him, and have changed the king's word, and yielded their bodies, that they might not serve nor worship any god, except their own God."*

The phrase, *'Who sent His Angel'* has been debated among Bible Scholars for many years as to whom this person was. It was impossible for the king to make with clarity as to who He was. However, many have thought that it was a Christophanies (an appearance of Jesus Christ). It may have been God in the person of the Holy Ghost. Whoever it was, He was greater than the fire of Babylon!

Not only did God deliver Shadrach, Meshach, and Abed-nego from the hand of the king, but, He delivered them with a fire greater than the god of fire Iz-bar. He also rendered the gods of Babylon the powerless!

This reminds me of the proclamation that John the Baptist made when speaking of Jesus Christ.

> *"I indeed baptize you with water unto repentance: but He that cometh after me is mightier than I, whose shoes I am not worthy to bear: He shall baptize you with the Holy Ghost, and with fire." Matt.3:11*

This fire is one that devours and removes the dross of sin in the life of the believing sinner.

> *"But ye shall receive power, after that the Holy Ghost is come upon you: Acts 1:1a*

> *"And suddenly there came a sound from heaven as of a rushing mighty wind, and it filled all the house where they were sitting."*

> *"And there appeared unto them cloven tongues like as fire, and it sat upon each of them."*
>
> *"And they all were filled with the Holy Ghost, and began to speak with other tongues, as the Spirit gave them utterance." Acts 2:2-4*

It is through the **'Cross and the finished Work of Jesus Christ'** the Satan and all his minions have been rendered powerless (Col. 2:14-15) by the **'Finished Work of Jesus Christ at Calvary!'** Then, by the Baptism in the Holy Ghost the believer can walk in the power and authority of the Holy Ghost which brings victory over sin and renders the enemy powerless! (Romans 6:4,14; Romans 8)

It is time for the believers to stand up and show forth the **'Power and Fire'** that Jesus Christ has provided!

The great Apostle Peter in his first Epistle deals with the **'fiery trials'** of the believer; While the great persecution of the church from the first empire-wide persecution (in A.D. 2490 had not yet taken place, Peter wrote this letter (in A.D. 60's) to encourage the believers to endure the intense persecution they were facing and that which was yet to come.

> *"Wherein ye greatly rejoice though for a season, if need be, ye are in heaviness through manifold temptations,"*
>
> *"That the trial of your faith, being much more precious than gold that perisheth, though it being tried with fire, might be found unto praise and honor and glory at the appearing of Jesus Christ." 1 Peter 1:6-7*

The phrase *"Wherein ye greatly rejoice"* refers to the state of mind and spirit of the believer while facing difficult times and situations. It is the attitude that one should have while being tested. It does not mean, **'rejoice'** for it, but to **'rejoice'** through it. James in his epistle uses the terminology that is similar when he said, *'Count it all joy when you fall into different types of trials.' James 1:2*

The phrase, *"though now for a season,"* comes with great encouragement for the believer. The word, **'Season'** is from the Greek word, **'Oligon'** meaning; little, small, few. This comes with the idea of, whatever you are facing will not last forever. While it may seem long term when facing difficult trials and test, it really is short term in comparison to the weight of glory! (2. Cor. 4:18). They day will come and my I say soon approaching when, *'Quickly approaching when Jesus Christ is coming back to rapture His church!' 1 Cor. 15:51-58; 1 Thess. 4:16-18*

The phrase, *"if need be,"* is one of great interest to me. The word, **'need'** is from the Greek word, **'Del'** meaning; must, necessary, by the nature of things. The reason this peaks my interest is because, it deals with each believer individually. It becomes necessary for some believers to face more trials and tests than others in order to fulfill God's purpose in their walk with Him. Every trial or test that originates from God is with the purpose pose to bring maturity and to equip the believer. There will be times when God will step back and allow Satan to bring temptations. However, even then it is a time in the class room for the believer to learn. The design is to bring discipline into the life of the believer.

The phrase, *"ye are in heaviness"* refers to being in a sorrowful position and or condition. Just living in this present world presents these kind of times. With that in mind, the believer can face these times with an abundant joy knowing, **'this too shall pass!'** Think on the terms, you are being prepared for a life of eternity where all the sorrows and pain of this day are passed away!

The phrase, *"through manifold temptations,'* the word, *'manifold'* refers to the diversity of trials and temptations. As referred to earlier, James in his epistle chapter 1:2 uses the word *divers,'* which, also refers to the diversity of trials and temptations the believer will face. It does not determine the amount but the diversity. In other words, trials, teats, and temptations come in different forms and fashions, from people, places, and things.

The word, *'Temptations,* is from the Greek word, *'Peirazo'* meaning; a putting to proof (by experiment [of good], experience [of evil], solicitation, discipline or provocation); by impl., adversity; temptation. Whether the test is from God, or a temptation from Satan, it is designed to reveal the character and or maturation of the believer.

The phrase, *'the trial of your faith'* refers to the testing of the believer within their faith, which reveals little or great faith. The different levels of Christian growth often determine the intensity of the trial or test. The word, *'trial'* is from the Greek word *'Dokimos'* meaning; the proving of, a criterion, test by which anything is proven or tried; for an example; faith can be tested by afflictions (James1:3; 1 Peter 1:7).

Testing also reveals where the believer is standing in his/her faith. It serves as a barometer which reveals the weakness, strengths, and stability of the believer (we all have weakness and areas that need strengthening). The greatest revelation in the believer being tested in their faith, is the showing of what and or who their faith is standing on!. It is a genuine faith? That being, a faith that is solely founded and established on the **'Cross and the Finished Work of Jesus Christ,' (Hebrews 12:2)** or is it another kind of faith? This is the question that we ask continually in the faith series **"Misplaced Faith!"**

The phrase, *'being much more precious than gold that periseth'* refers to true faith being established within the heart and mind of the believer, which is in the, **'Cross and what 'Jesus Christ there did,'** Notice the following quote;

> *"The Lord does not willingly afflict, yet His wise love often appoints sharp trials, to show His people their hearts, and to do them good at the latter end. And the trial of faith is more precious than the gold; in both there is purification, separation of dross, and discovery of soundness and goodness. But gold does not increase and multiply when tried by fire, it becomes less; while faith in fire is established, improved, and multiplied, by oppositions and afflictions; gold must perish at last, and can only purchase perishing things, while the trial of faith will be found to praise, and honor, and glory."*

Matthew Henry's Commentary on 1 Peter 1:7

The phrase, *'though it be tried with fire,'* the word, is from the Greek word, **'Dikimazo'** meaning; to try, discern, distinguish, approve. It has the notion of proving a thing whether it be worthy to be received.

Even though faith is more precious than gold, that is not the intent of what the Apostle Peter is saying. Peter is referring the process of trials presenting the believer as walking in genuine faith. And once again, that faith is in the **"Cross and the Finished Work of Jesus Christ!"**

The trial of your faith is like a crucible, which is a severe test. It is a pot used to purify a thing. The main purpose of faith being tried is to prove whether it is genuine or not. God does not just accept any kind of faith. Pure, unadulterated faith is a faith that has its object in the **'Cross and the Finished Work of Jesus Christ!'** Any other kind of faith is missing the mark and is not acceptable to God. Matter of fact, without faith having the correct object, how can anyone receive salvation? The answer is an astounding, **"they can't!'**

The phrase, ***"unto praise, and honor and glory at the appearing of Jesus Christ"*** is referring to the results of faith being tried and all impurities exposed and removed. The results are presented to Jesus Christ at the rapture of His Church!

With all of this in mind, you, the believer, should rejoice and count it all joy when facing trails and tests. I am not suggesting being joyful for the test, however, the rejoicing should be in the fact that you and I are found worthy to be tested, and that true, pure faith is the results! **So, Rejoice and again I say Rejoice and Keep The Faith!**

CHAPTER 6

Jesus Testing the Disciples
In the Storm

In the previous chapter we talked about **'faith being tried by fire.'** In this chapter we are going to look at faith being tested from a different perspective. Jesus Christ tested the faith of His disciples in several different ways. We are going to look at a couple of them.

<u>Testing in the Storm!</u>

I have always been amazed at storms. Storms are something that we can relate to on one level or another. Some storms are more devastating than others. However, going through any type of storms, be that physically or spiritually, changes us. I can remember as a child watching a tornado making a path through a field next to our home. I could see it clear enough to observe some of the objects that were within it.

In the middle seventies I was pasturing a church in a small town in Florida when a hurricane came bellowing through. The tall pine trees around would bend and sway with the gusting of the winds. There was a huge oak tree in our front yard that was only a few feet from our dwelling. That huge oak tree stood tall and unmoved by the winds of that storm, it only lost a few small dead branches, which needed to be removed any way. While observing the storm and what was taking place, I learned a great lesson. Concerning the personal storms we face in life. I learned that it is how we react (respond) to the storms that makes the difference. Whether we are the tall pine trees bending and swaying or the great oak tree that stood tall and firm, we can survive the storms of life!

As I said before, it is how we react (respond) to the storms that determines a positive or negative outcome. When you talk to people who have been through a rough storm and have learned from it, you get the sense of respect for the storm. When facing a storm you can learn something by how you reacted. Often times, those who are in the midst of a storm, when they stay calm and do not panic make better decisions which can keep them from serious injury. There is a lesson to be learned in every storm we face and that lesson can be shared with others. To make the correct and effective decisions while in a storm can bring you health and longevity. Notice the following questions from a great friend and pastor.

We need to ask ourselves the question; **"How do we handle the storms of life?" "Are we looking for the blessings after the storms of life?"** Source; Pastor Tim Agee, The Sanctuary Church, Indianapolis/Beech Grove.

The scriptures give reference over sixty times to the weather and storms. Out of those sixty times, the scripture uses some forty times as comparison to the storms we face in life.

<u>There Is A Purpose For Every Storm You (We) Face!</u>

1. <u>Think of the storm (the flood) in Genesis 6-8.</u>

The purpose of this storm was to cleanse and purify the earth from the wickedness of man.

2. <u>God Used A Storm To Get Jonah In His Proper Place</u>.!

This storm was used to bring back focus and direction. There are times in our life when we need to re-focus and have clear direction.

3. <u>The Disciples Were Put In The Middle Of A Storm That Changed Their Thinking And Their Faith!</u>

This storm was a teaching tool to keep one's faith focused on Jesus Christ. We will examine in greater detail this particular storm within the following pages.

4. <u>Storms Will Also Reveal How God Is In Control Of Our Surrounding Circumstances And Turmoil. (Psalm 107)</u>

There is little doubt that God uses the storms of life as a teaching tool. It teaches for one to place all of his/her faith and trust in the **'Cross and the Finished Work of Jesus Christ!** Storm will also reveal the blessings in which Jesus Christ has provided.

The storm you may be facing is not for your destruction, but for your growth and maturation. When you (we) learn to keep **'The Faith'** while in the middle of a storm you (we) are on our way to **"VICTORY!'**

Let's examine a storm that Jesus used to test the faith of His disciples.

> *"And straightway, Jesus constrained His disciples to get in a ship, and to go before Him unto the other side, while He sent the multitudes away."*

1. <u>JESUS PUT HIS DISCIPLES IN THE STORM.</u>

There are some very interesting within the above passage of scripture. The disciples had just been involved in a great miracle where there were five thousand men, and that is not counting the women and children. The multitude was served a meal that came from five loaves and two fishes and they did all eat until they were filled (Matt. 14:20). Upon everyone being filled, the disciples gathered up twelve baskets full of the leftovers. **What a miracle!**

From here Jesus sent His disciples away while He sent the multitudes away. Notice, Jesus had to **'constrain'** the disciples to get into the ship. The word **'constrain'** is very interesting, it comes from the Greek word, **'Anagkazo'** which is from, *'anagke'* meaning necessity; to force, compel, by importunate (urgent or persistent in asking or demanding) persuasion. There may be several reasons why Jesus had to constrain his disciples to get into the ship. I am convinced, the disciples were concerned about getting out on the water because they could see a storm approaching. If you have ever been out to sea and experience a storm you could certainly understand their concern.

There was a statement made by Jesus, which, I believe was missed by His disciples. He (Jesus) said, *"Go before me unto the other side."* **'You may be asking, what is so important by that statement?' 'What did they miss' When Jesus said,** *"go before me unto the other side,"* **this meant that no matter what they would face they would arrive on the other side!**

You may be in the midst of a great storm, but, may I say, **"You will make it through!** One of the mistakes that the disciples made (which believers often make), They began to focus on the storm and lost sight of what Jesus had spoke to them, (that may sound familiar). Too often we allow the (our) outside circumstances to dictate how we feel and how we respond to a given situation. Storms in life are not meant for your destruction but for a blessing! While facing your particular storm remember, you are not alone, the Holy Spirit ids ever present with you!

While being in the perfect will of what Jesus was having them to do (His disciples), they were placed within a storm. As I said, you are not alone when you are in the middle of a storm!. While in the storm take the opportunity to **'learn deeper trust and faith in Jesus Christ!'**

2. <u>WHILE IN THE STORM JESUS CONTINUED TO WATCH OVER HIS DISCIPLES!</u>

> *"But the ship was now in the midst of the sea, tossed with waves; for the sea was contrary."*
> *Matt. 14:24*

> *"And He (Jesus) saw them (the disciples) toiling in rowing; for the wind was contrary."*
> *Mark 6:48a*

Jesus was aware of where the disciples were and what was happening. He was aware of the storm they were in just, as He is aware of the storms you (the believer) face in your life. Remember, He (Jesus Christ) is your shepherd and He is continually watching over you (Psalm 23). Not only is He watching over you, He is seeing and. understanding how you are reacting in the storm. When it is too much for you to handle and the storm is overwhelming you, **HE (JESUS CHRIST) WILL SHOW UP!**

3. <u>HE WILL SHOW UP IN YOUR STORM!</u>

> *"And in the fourth watch (between 3 a.m. and 6 a.m.) Jesus went unto them, walking on the water."*

> *"And when the disciples saw Him walking on the sea, they were troubled, saying, It is a spirit; and cried out for fear." Matt. 14:25-26*

> *"And about the fourth watch of the night He cometh unto them, walking upon he sea, and would have passed by them."*

> *"But when they saw Him walking upon the sea, they supposed it had been a spirit, and cried out." Mark 6:48b-49*

In hindsight (which is always 20/20) it is amazing to me that after being involved in the miracle of feeding five thousand men with just five loaves and two fishes and yet they did not recognize Jesus coming to them. I really should not be surprised, when the Church of today is doing the s.ame thing. We allow fear and doubt to dictate to us when storms arrive. At the time of this writing we are in the midst of a 'Pandemic' which (along with the news media) has created fear. In my fifty years of ministry I have never seen Christians (believers) fall into this terrible trap. Any time we give more attention to the storm and we do to the **'Cross and the finished Work of Jesus Christ'** fear and doubt will rush in!

Just as Jesus was aware of the disciples and their limits and fears, He is aware of yours also. Where ever you may be at this time and whatever you are facing, **'Don't ever forget, Jesus Christ will show!** He always shows up at the right time! You may be in one of the darkest times of your life, but, be of good courage, for God is in the midst working out good for you!

> *"And we know that all things work together for good to them that love God, to them who are called according to His purpose." Romans 8:28*

<u>LESSONS TO LEARN FROM YOUR STORM!</u>

It is important to learn some valuable lessons from any storm. I have looked back at some of the stormy times in my life, and after looking at them closely I could see the lesson I needed. You may be thinking, *"Dr. Baldock, you just don't understand what I am facing or where I have come from."* You are exactly right, so, within the next few page we are going to show you just how to look at that terrible storm in into **'God's Gracious Victory!**

A. Jesus Christ knows exactly where you are!

B. He knows your limitations!

C. He will show up in your darkest hour!

D. There is comfort in your storm when all of your trust and faith is in the 'Cross and the Finished Work of Jesus Christ!

E. Your storm can be the starting point of a miracle!

4. <u>STORM PRESENT OPPORTUNITIES FOR SPIRITUAL GROWTH!</u>

While in this storm Peter received a revelation of having good courage, which literally changed his life. Peter was given an opportunity to leave his comfort zone (getting out of the ship) and put all his trust and Faith in Jesus Christ for God is in the midst working out good for you!

"And we know that all things work together for good to them that love God, to them who according to His purpose." Romans 8:28

"But straightway Jesus spoke unto them, saying; Be of good cheer; it is I; be not afraid."

"And Peter answered Him and said, Lord, if it be thou, bid me come unto thee on the water."

"And He (Jesus) said, Come And when Peter was come down out of the ship, he walked on water to Jesus."

"But when he saw the wind boisterous, he was afraid: beginning to sink, he cried, saying, Lord, save me."

"And immediately Jesus stretched forth His hand, and caught him, and said unto him, O thou of little faith, wherefore didst thou doubt?"
Matt. 14:28-31

After reading the above passage, one might say, "Peter failed and began to sink!" You are exactly right, however, while sinking he cried out to Jesus to save him. When that great hand of Jesus Christ was extended to him he found a whole new level of comfort and peace.

Like everything we face in life there should be some kind of lesson to learn. In this case, is a tremendous lesson as to why Peter began sinking. As I have stated before, when we (The believer) begin to focus on what is going on around (the severity of the storm) and take our eyes off of the, **'Cross and the Finished Work of Jesus Christ'** we are in trouble. Thank God, Peter had enough sense to call on the one who could and would save him. It is also interesting to note, **'Jesus was in the storm with Him!**

With that being said, it is also important to understand that through the storms that we face in life, they will often bring spiritual growth. Again, the believer can grow spiritually and receive great revelation form the storms!

A. <u>Storms reveal areas in the life of the believer that needs to change!</u>

Every believer has certain things they need to improve on and some things that they need to get rid of. It does not matter who you are nor does your status quo come into the equation. Nobody walking this earth is perfect, contrary to what some people may think. And no one knows everything, we all need work. We may be a new creature in Christ (2 Cor. 5:17) however, we are still a work in progress.

I can recall going through a certain experience (storm) in which I allowed bitterness to take hold. That bitterness did not come alone, he brought his pals of anger, spite, and un-forgiveness. It took me several years along with t he conviction of the Holy Spirit for me to get rid of that junk. Thank. God, I am free today! Getting free from all of the bitterness, anger, spite and lack of forgiveness was not an easy road to travel. Matter of fact, my deliverance did not happen overnight. It took me years to finally face up to the root of my problem, which was, withholding forgiveness. I thought I was justified in feeling the way I did. The Holy Spirit continually worked on me, and it was like the peeling of an onion, taking layer by layer until the root was exposed. That particular storm revealed a problem that I did think I had. Matter of fact, God has used many storms in my life as a schoolmaster. There is one great thing about storms being a schoolmaster you will not forget them and you will not desire to go through that storm again!

B. <u>Storms reveals our weaknesses!</u>

No matter how strong a person may think they are, there are still areas of weakness that we must face and allow the Holy Spirit to work on us. As long as the sin nature resides in us (in the believer) there will always be something that we must work on (peel away like an onion)! In the last several years there have been few days that the Holy Spirit has not spoke to me concerning some kind of change or weakness that need to be removed. The removing of any type of weakness comes with disciple and spiritual exercise. The Apostle Peter reveals the kind of spiritual exercises we (the believer) must do in order to overcome the weaknesses of the flesh. He also reveals the principles that are needed in order to walk and live within the **'Divine Nature of Jesus Christ!' (2 Peter 1:1-10)**

C. <u>Storms will reveal one's true character!</u>

It is when our back is to the wall that true character shows its ugly face! If you want to find out where you are in your walk with Jesus Christ, let there be a storm! When in the midst of a storm ask yourself these questions; 'How do I or did I react when I was in the storm?' 'Was there a character change in me while I was in the storm?' Sometimes certain people and things can be a storm within itself. For an example; 'How do you manage your emotions while driving in traffic?' How about when someone cuts you off in traffic?' How about when someone gets up in your face and uses certain language they think describes you?' Sometimes it is not easy to walk away from those kind of storms (yes, those are storms)! These kinds of situations often bring out old man's anger. How should we handle that old man?

I realize the scriptures declare for the believer to *'anger and sin not!*

> *"Be ye angry and sin not: let the sun go down upon your wrath." Eph. 4:26*

The only anger that meets God's approval is *'Righteous anger.'* **'Righteous Anger,'** is to be angry at what angers God, and that is sin. It is not an anger that brings harm. It is important to understand, becoming angry is a choice, and that it is coming from the emotions of the *'sin nature.'* This is one the many reasons why it is important for the believer to renew their mind on a daily basis. (Ro. 12:2)

The only way to control one's emotions (including anger) is to allow the Holy Spirit the latitude to work within us (the believer) See Romans chapter eight which reveals the *'Dynamics of the Holy Spirit!'* The Apostle Peter is a great example of one who was taught a lesson concerning his temper (anger) (John 18:10-11)

5. <u>Jesus Christ will see you through the storm!</u>

Just as Jesus was mindful of His disciples in their storm, so is He mindful of your current storm.

> *"And when even was come, the ship was in the midst of the sea, and He alone on the land."*

> *"And He (Jesus) saw them toiling in rowing; for the wind was contrary unto them; about the fourth watch of the night He (Jesus) cameth*

unto them, walking upon the sea, and would have passed by them."

"But when they saw Him (Jesus) walking upon the sea, they supposed it had been a spirit."
Mark 6:47-49

The phrase, *"And He saw them toiling in rowing."* This indicates two very important elements.

1. **Jesus saw them (He was mindful) of their toiling (rowing in their own strength and ability).** As we made mentioned earlier in the chapter **Jesus saw (He was mindful) of their situation within the storm.** It is of great comfort to know and understand that Jesus Christ is **'mindful'** of whatever storm you may be facing. Jesus also was mindful that the disciples were rowing against the wind and sea within their own strength and ability. There comes a time when we need to stopped struggling and operating in our own ability and become strong in the Lord!

2. **He (Jesus) came walking upon the sea toward His disciples.** This is also important to take notice of. The disciples were so caught up in the storm that they failed to recognize that it was Jesus coming toward them.

   "But when they saw Him walking upon the sea, they supposed it had been a spirit, and cried out." Mark 6:49

This part of the story has always amazed me. How is it, that the disciples were just involved in a great miracle feeding five thousand women and children with five loaves and two fishes and yet, did not recognize the **'miracle worker?'** I say that, yet, it becomes so easy for the believer today to focus on their particular storm that they can become blinded to the presences of Jesus Christ.

It is when we allow surrounding circumstances to become so overwhelming, that we can lose sight of Jesus being in the storm with us! Their focus on the storm opened the door for fear and unbelief to rush in. This is what I refer to as, **'living from the outside in rather than the inside out!'** What I mean by that statement is, when we allow outside circumstances to dictate how we feel on the inside. I am certainly not making light of your past or present situations however, you can be assured that Jesus Christ is in the middle of your current storm (situation)!

> *"And we know that all things work together for good to them that love God, to them that are called according to His purpose." Romans 8:28*

3. Jesus came to them within the storm.

> *"For they all saw Him, and were troubled. And immediately He talked with them, and saith unto them, Be of good cheer: it is I; be not afraid.*

Years ago a preached a message entitled, **'There is a Yes in the Middle of Your Mess!'** The problem can be, we can't see the **'Yes'** because of the mess (the storm)! Be reminded of the following;

> *"Our soul waiteth for the Lord: He is our help and our shield." Psalm 33:20*

*"Take hold of shield and buckler,, and stand up
for mine help" Psalm. 35:2*

*"God is our refuge and strength, a very present
help in trouble." Psalm 46:1*

4. Jesus Spoke to Them In the Storm.

Upon seeing and hearing Jesus, Peter spoke up and said;

*"And Peter answered Him and said, Lord, if it
be thou, bid me come unto thee on the water."*

*"And He said, Come. And when Peter was come
down out of the ship, he walked on the water, to
go Jesus." Matt 14:28-29*

It was by faith and the spoken Word of Jesus Christ that gave
Peter the strength and ability to get up out of the ship and to
walk on the water! It is when the believer is able to put faith
and trust within the Word of God that great things happen. You
may be thinking, **'Yes, but Peter began to sink!'** You are right.
However, before we begin to criticize Peter (which becomes
easy to do) look at what he did do.

A. When Jesus spoke, he (Peter) got out of the ship.

**B. When he began to sink he cried out for the Lord to
save him.**

C. Jesus then stretched for His hand and caught him."

I have to admit, it is somewhat puzzling that Peter acted on the Word, **'Come,'** and then took his eyes off of Jesus and looked once again, at the storm. The good news is, he knew, Who to call upon for help! Peter did receive a rebuke from Jesus, *'O ye of little (brief, puny) faith wherefore didst thou doubt?'*

Just as many believers toady, it can become so easy for Peter to take his eye of faith off of Jesus and focus on the problem surrounding him. This severs as a reminder, that, we must have the right object of faith before us; **'Our faith must continually be focused on the Cross and the Finished Work of Jesus Christ!'** When this is your (our) focus you (we) can face our daily living with the assurance that Jesus Christ has **'Got This!'** When you find yourself in the middle of a storm and that feeling of helplessness and or hopelessness begins to come upon you, remember, He, Jesus Christ, is in the storm with you! Just call upon **'His Name,'** and He will answer! I guarantee you by the **'Word of God'** that He will show up and show out, just for you!

You can be assured without any doubt nor unbelief, that Jesus is ever present with you! The great Apostle Paul declared:

"Jesus Christ the same yesterday, and to day, and forever."
Hebrews 13:8

While going through dark and stormy times, we (the believer) are presented with an opportunity to step out in faith and receive the miracle Jesus has provided us through the **'Cross!'**

<u>Think on the following:</u>

1. **If you are facing a storm today.**

2. If you are feeling like you are sinking and possibly cannot make it through.

3. Now is the time to focus all of your faith, hope and trust in Jesus Christ and what He accomplished at Calvary!

4. Now is the time to embrace the Blessings that are within the Storm.

Pastor Tim Agee Sanctuary Church Beech Grove/ Indianapolis , Indiana

CHAPTER 7

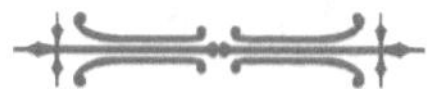

The Ultimate Test

When I look through the scriptures and examine the many trials and tests I am convince that the ultimate test has to do with Abraham and his son Isaac. Imagine, after waiting some twenty –five years and watching your body and the body of Sarah go beyond the ability to produce children then, through your inability along with Sarah's womb being dead, God give you the promised child **(Romans 4:17-25)**

From the time that God first spoke to Abraham his life consisted of one kind of test after another. On the surface, these many tests may seem to be anything but fair. However, as we have made mentioned before, **'a faith not tested is a faith not trusted!'** Before we examine the **'ultimate test'** for Abraham let's look into some other things that God required of this great man.

In Genesis 12, after God spoke to Abram and told him that he was going to be the **'father of many nations,' (Gen. 12:3)** for the next twenty-five years (Abram who became Abraham) lived in hope with **'Anticipation'** of the beginning of God's promise!

The moment God spoke to Abram, faith came up within and he began his journey to become the **'Father of many nations!'** His journey, which was not always easy, and he made some bad decisions of the way. However, he never let go of the faith that was placed within him! The blessings God promised; **first came the instructions of separation!**

<u>Separation!</u>

1. **He was to separate himself from his country!**

2. **He was to separate himself from his kindred!**

3. **He was to separate himself his father's house!**

When faith and anticipation become a team, it will require a life of separation!

<u>The Blessings Promised!</u>

1. **God would make Abram a great Nation! Gen. 12:2**

2. **God will make Abram's name great! Gen. 12:2**

3. **Abram will be a blessing! Gen. 12:2**

4. **God will bless those that bless Him ! Gen. 12:3**

5. **God will curse those that curse him (Abram) Gen. 12:3**

6. **In Abram all the families of the Earth will be blessed! Gen. 12:3**

It was then that Abram separated himself and departed in **'faith'** and began to live a life of **'anticipation!**

The faith and anticipation of Abram (Abraham) is revealed in his walk with God! He (Abraham) was required to also surrender (separate) himself in seven prominent areas, the last of which I refer to as the **'Ultimate Test!'**

1. **He surrendered his own country**

2. **He surrendered his family**

3. **He surrendered the way of Jordan. Gen. 13:14-18**

4. **He surrendered the riches of Sodom. Gen. 14:21-24**

5. **He surrendered himself. Gen. 15:7-17**

6. **He surrendered Ishmael. Gen. 21:7-14**

7. **He surrendered Isaac. Gen. 22:1-14**

Upon the final separation God confirmed His Covenant with Abraham. With every separation Abraham was increased in spiritual knowledge and wealth. The same is true for every believer today. The more we separate ourselves from the world and separate ourselves to God the greater we grow and become **'Spiritually wealthy!"**

Further proof that Abraham lived in faith and anticipation;

1. **When against hope he yet believed in hope! Ro. 4:18**

2. **Was no weak in his faith! Ro. 4:19**

3. **He did not consider the age of his own body, neither, did he consider the deadness of Sarah's Ro. 4:19**

4. **He did not stagger (waver) at the promises of God. Ro. 4:20**

5. **He did not allow unbelief, but was strong in faith, giving glory to God! Ro. 4:20**

6. **He was fully persuaded in what God promised. Ro. 4:21**

I am convinced beyond any doubt, the mindset of faith and anticipation of Abraham is a model of how the believer of today is to think and walk with God!

The Test of Tests!

"And it came to pass after these things, that God did tempt Abraham, and said unto him, Abraham; and he said, Behold, here am I."

"And He (God) said, Take now thine only son Isaac, whom thou lovest, and get thee into the land of Moriah; and offer him (Isaac) there for a burnt offering upon one of the mountains which I will tell thee of." Gen. 22:1-2

The phrase, **"after these things"** the question is, **after what things?"** This is referring to several years after the expulsion of Ishmael. Isaac would possibly be somewhere between the ages of 20 and 30. The rabbinical tradition has Isaacs at 37 when he was bound.

Abraham's response to God, **"Behold, here I am"** is better translated **"behold me!'** It is Abraham availed himself to God, for whatever God wants and desires of him! I am certain that this great Patriarch was not totally aware of what he was about to face. However, it was not unusual for God to call upon Abraham, however, this call would be like none other.

There are several phrases within the above passage of scripture that is in need of a deeper study. The phrase, *"that God did tempt Abraham."* is from the Hebrew word, 'Nasah' meaning; to test, try, prove, put to the proof. In most places this verb carries with it the idea of testing the quality of someone or something through a demonstration of stress. At the time the KJV was translated (1611), to **"tempt"** meant to **"test,"** rather than the current meaning of **"enticing to do wrong."** God does not tempt man (James1:13), the rendering of **"tempt"** for **"nasah"** in Gen. 22:1 became a problem and would have better been translated, **"to test or prove!"**

In the testing of Abraham God was refining the character of Abraham, He continues to do so with every believer of today.

As I made mentioned in an earlier chapter, God's testing of the believer is not to prove to Him (God) who or where the believer is in their faith but rather for the benefit of the believer to know and understand where they stand in their faith. Once again, **'Faith must be tested, for a faith that is not tested is a faith that cannot be trusted! The greater the faith, the greater the test!**

<u>Why This Kind of Test?</u>

Because of the actions of Adam, sin was introduced into the world. Due to Adam's disobedience (sin) the world has been in chaotic state one of which caused enmity between God and man. God had to bring redemption to Adam's fallen race. This could only happen by God becoming man which was decided before the foundation of the world (1 Peter 1:18-20). While the first Adam failed miserably, the last Adam (Jesus Christ) brought redemption (1 Cor. 15:45). Abraham would play a major role in bringing the redeemer into the world! Within this great test of Abraham is the revelation of the redemptive act of God!

It is important to realize that Satan had nothing to do with this great test, it was God and God alone and for a great reason. The following example of Abraham's test reveals the great price that had to be paid for the redemption of man! And that great price was Jesus Christ being crucified and raised from the dead! Since God cannot die He had to become Man in order to complete the great plan of redemption. **(John 1:1-14)**

> *"And He said, Take now your son, your only son,*
> *whom you love, and get into the land of Moriah;*
> *and offer him therefore a Burnt Offering upon one*
> *of the mountains which I will tell you." Gen. 22:2*

I just image about this time that Abraham's heart dropped (mine certainly would have). The phrase, *"Take now your son, your only son"* is interesting. The word, **'only'** is unique and it is referring specifically to Isaac, and the reference is **'one-of-a-kind.** Isaac became a type of Jesus Christ, God's **'only'** Son who He loved.

The phrase, *"whom you love"* is interesting in the fact that this is the first time the word **'love'** is mentioned in scripture. It implies an ardent and vehement inclination of the mind and a tenderness of affection at the same time. It reveals the close attachment between parents and their children.

The word, *'Moriah'* means; *'Jah or Jehovah is Provider!'*

This command (test) from God put Abraham in the following positions;

1. <u>Abraham had to decide if he was really hearing from God.</u>

Abraham's decision had to be one of clarity, for, a human sacrifice was something that was abhorrent to God. Let me stop here for a moment and clarify something. I am in no way suggesting that God would ever present this kind of test today. This was for a specific time and purpose! Again, Abraham had to decide if he was hearing from God. I have no doubt that Abraham knew the voice of God, as he and God had conversed on many occasions. Matter of fact, this would be the seventh surrender.

2. <u>The Test Intensifies;</u>

Abraham was being told to sacrifice his son in whom God had promised to be his seed. This request had to be somewhat of a jolt to Abraham. However, I am convinced that Abraham's faith in God ran so deep, that even though his thoughts may have been many, he was convinced in his faith. My conclusion is drawn from the following passages of scripture;

> *"And Abraham rose up early in the morning,*
> *and saddled his ass, and took two of his young*
> *men with him, and Isaac his son, and clave the*
> *wood for the burnt offering, and rose up, and*
> *went unto the place which God had told him."*
> *Gen. 22:3*

The phrase, ***"And Abraham rose up early in the morning,"*** indicates that Abraham began immediately in obedience to what God had spoken unto him. This is an interesting point. I have noticed over the years that all it takes is one glimpse of hesitation in faith opens the door for the enemy to introduce doubt and unbelief. Abraham's immediate obedience reveals the great faith he had in God. Further evidence of the depth of Abraham's faith is noted within the following scripture;

> *"Then on the third day Abraham lifted up his*
> *eyes, ad saw the place afar off."*

> *"And Abraham said unto his young men, Abide*
> *here with the ass; and I and the lad will go*
> *yonder and worship and come again unto you."*
> *Gen. 22:4-5*

The phrase, ***"the lad and I will go yonder and worship"*** is a very interesting statement. This is the first time the word ***worship'*** is used in scripture and it comes from the Hebrew word. ***'Shachah'*** meaning; to depress; to prostrate oneself (in homage to royalty or to God. It especially is used in the worship of deity. Therefore it meant to honor God with prayers. Brother Jimmy Swaggart states in his Expositor's Study Bible;

> *"praise is what we do, while worship is what we are; every part and particle of our life and living should be worship of the Lord; while all worship is not praise, all praise is definitely worship; this is the first time the word "worship" is used in the Bible."*

Everything the believer does and faces should be done with *"worship"* unto the Lord! Worship must be the lifestyle of the believer!

The phrase *"and come again to you"* revealed the depth of Abraham's faith included, **'God raising Isaac from the dead!'**

> *"By faith Abraham, when he was tried, offered up Isaac: and he that received the promises offered up his only begotten son."*

> *"Of whom it was said, That in Isaac shall thy seed be called;"*

> *"Accounting that God was able to raise him up, even from the dead; from whence also he received him in a figure." Hebrews 11:17-19*

I think it is perfectly clear, that even when God stopped Abraham from offering Isaac (Gen. *22:9-13),* Abraham had counted it done. **'What a man of faith!'** Not only did Abraham exhibit strong faith, but he revealed just how strong he was in his faith! Abraham held onto the promises of God when God said, Isaac would be the seed of Abraham. I am convinced that God revealed to Abraham His great plan of redemption! This very act required of Abraham was a foreshadowing of how God was going redeem mankind. Redemption was to come in the order of God sacrificing **'His Only Begotten Son at Calvary!'**

The phrase, ***"he received him in a figure"*** is from the Greek, and is saying, ***'and figuratively speaking, he received Isaac back from the dead.'*** Abraham knew that the Redeemer would come through Isaac!

There are some other interesting statements within this great story.

> ***"And Isaac spake unto Abraham his father, and said, my father: And he said, here am I, my son. And he said, behold the fire and the wood: but where is the Lamb for a burnt offering?"***
>
> ***"And Abraham said, my son, God will provide Himself a lamb for a burnt offering: so they went both of them." Gen. 22:7-8***

What an answer, Abraham gave to Isaac, ***"God will provide Himself a lamb for a burnt offering!"*** What a statement of faith! Could it be possible that God allowed Abraham to look forward and see the **'True Sacrificial Lamb of God?'** I personally believe that it was very possible. Think about the depth of Abraham's statement, **'God will provide Himself a Lamb!'** I do believe that Abraham saw the provision of God for man's redemption. What a great test for a great Patriarch. I am certainly not suggesting that this test was in any way easy for Abraham. However, when you consider the faith of Abraham and the hand of God throughout this process, Abraham surely saw the outcome!

Temptations, trials and tests may differ in their intensity. However, it has been proven time and time again when pure faith comes to the surface, victory is won! I will take a test from God, above any temptations from Satan. That being said, **'Spiritual Growth and Maturity in within every test is essential!**

George Williams said: ***"It is a higher honor to be tested by God. There are various kinds of trials, some from circumstances or some from the hand of Satan, but the highest character of a trial is that which comes from God Himself."***

CONCLUSION!

Trials, Temptations and Tests are given, and no one is exempt. It is not the trial, temptation or tests, that decides the outcome, it is you! The choices and decisions you make while facing each trial, temptation and test will determine the outcome! James said;

> *"My brethren, count it all joy when ye fall into divers (different manners) temptations."'*

> *"Knowing this, that the trying of your faith worketh patience."*

> *"But let patience have her perfect work, that ye maybe perfect and entire, wanting nothing."*
> *James 1:2-4*

<u>Your Faith Will Be Tested!</u>

<u>So, Holdfast In Your Faith! (Hebrews 10:23; 35-38</u>

<u>Don' Grow Weary In Well Doing! (Gal. 6:9)</u>

<u>Everything You Face, Face It With Faith In The Cross and The Finished Work of Jesus Christ! When Doing So, You Will Become A Well Rounded mature Christian (Child of God)!</u>

ABOUT THE AUTHOR

Dr. Baldock is the founder/ president of ***"Gaining the Victory Ministries."*** He began his ministry in March of 1971. In 1973, he began in full time ministry. He is celebrating the beginning of fifty years of ministry. He and his wife, Julie, have been married for thirty-six years. Together, they have seven grown children, Rick, Tammy, Tracy, Rhonda, Alicia, Michael, and Ashley. He and Julie have several grandchildren and great-grandchildren.

Dr. Baldock has pastored nine Churches; four of which he pioneered and built from the ground up. Dr. Baldock also has four earned Doctorate Degrees, and one Doctorate.

He is currently traveling to different church's teaching and preaching the Word of God. He attends the Sanctuary Church in Beech Grove/ Indianapolis, Indiana. Dr. Baldock has spoken at many different venues. He has worked with several well-known ministries. He taught for several years with the International College of Bible Theology and with Midwest Seminary. He has taught undergraduate and graduate school. He also taught at the School of the Prophets in Poplar Bluff, Missouri for about four years and he taught about two to three years at The Lion of Judah in Malden, Missouri. He also traveled to Malawi in East Africa where he helped train over one-hundred and twenty-five church leaders.

Dr. Baldock is a gifted preacher and teacher of the Word. He enjoys training up leaders in the local church and helping restore those who have fallen on hard times and are in need of mentoring. He has authored many books and study helps. He believes that the gifts God has given him should be shared and imparted to others. He believes in everyday, practical teaching which will reveal the application of the Word of God in the everyday living. He is a strong believer in the fact that everything you will ever need is supplied through **'The Cross and the finished work of Jesus Christ.'** He believes that the **'Cross'** is the means and **'Jesus Christ'** is the source of all that you have need of.

Dr. Baldock is available to speak and or teach at your local church or, conference, along with leadership training. If you would like for Dr. Baldock to come and speak at your church or conference, and if you would like more information about his books, cd's, dvd's, and teaching tools you can get in touch with him at;

Gaining The Victory Ministries
Dr. R. Michael Baldock
P.O. Box 648
Spencer, Indiana 47460;

You can email us at
gainingvictoryministries@gmail.com

Or visit our web page at
GTVministries.com

Or at;
gainingvictoryministries.org